CONTENTS

Though she would not have appreciated it,
this collection is dedicated to
Stephanie May
And to those who, sadly, would:
Margaret Cornish, Simon Wood, Maurice James,
Margaret Munro Gibson; and Dorothy May

4

WHERE THE LIVING IS EASY

i (Parked in a Lay-By)

There is something to be grateful for,
parked in a lay-by,
watching the world whoosh by,
waiting for a recovery vehicle

that doesn't come
and a husband that doesn't
   on this occasion.

Except, the job's been farmed out
to a local company
that will arrive; eventually.

The car rocks
every time a vehicle passes in the fast lane.
They all pass in the fast lane,
as I'm rocking in a lay-by
to nowhere.
There is something to be grateful for,
parked in a lay-by,
watching the world whoosh by:
a complement of mature trees,
no nettles
and full screening;
what a relief.

ii (Fuelled to Stop)

Men never would, would they?
It has to be women,
always women.
Because men never would, never could
possibly get it so wrong.

Men would not notice the sun
beaming down unforgivingly,
the brush of blue
and perfect whispering clouds.

Men could not possibly notice
verdant green cambering in density
beyond the lay-by,
in the beech trees;
and daisies large as cows' eyes
with fetching yellow pupils.

Because men never would, would they,
forget the junction, roundabout,
motorway crossing,
direction, distance or duration?

Men may quote every feminine shape
with an engine,
colour, year,

but they never would, would they,
forget to fill up the car
with barely a thought.

Except, they know who drives what,
how fast; which driver's pushy,
testosterone-fuelled.

So how can a woman recover
from the indignity
of filling the car with unleaded
instead of diesel;
because a man never would...

iii (Sat Nav)

There are two lay-bys
and a magpie brings the only colour,
brazenly crossing the dual carriageway.

There are two bins,
one in each lay-by
and the car rocks every time
a van storms through.

And nothing's stopped in the southbound
since the white van driver,
puffing on his cigarette,
rudely awakened
by a distraught woman
asking what road they were on?

And the Sat Nav never lies
and yet, and yet
no-one could find the location
for breakdown recovery.

No police cars,
no recovery services;
just endless speeding motorists and
-give them their due- they tried,
the mobile ringing every five minutes
and how they all tried to help,
for the Sat Nav never lies.
Thank goodness for a mobile signal.

iv (Where the Living is Easy)

A hard time I've had of it
and yet it was all about arriving
and not the journey,
although there was a journey of sorts
that's spread spectacularly in the telling.

Yet was I bursting to tell?
No, for it was deathly.
Yet, set down
this, set down
this. There was a pub of sorts,
I had evidence and no doubt.
At the bar, in the snug,
or grouped around each table.

They were all here – locals –
after a day where the living is easy
as Dartmoor
in the country
beside the gorge
and whether this was burst a gut, or deathly,
there was everything to see and hear;
and the wait for steak and ale pie?

Easy.

v (The Farm)

There are sheep enough
in the fields; or cows.
And everywhere shows remnants
of a modern farm.

This is a path;
that a seat or mushroom;
there an old plough,
rusty for authenticity.

The pigs in the pen are real,
sleeping off a hard day's snuffles
and the breakfast will be full English
in a few hours,
when pub fayre has settled like a sty
or there is time enough and light
to explore junior farm.

But set down
this. Set down
this.

There is no human being
in sight or earshot
and I would give anything to hear
the old man snoring.

vi (Early Morning) (Triolet)

No stars are in the sky,
no eerie owls in flight,
no foxes flaming by,
no stars are in the sky.
The geese are cackling, high,
fluffed cockerels peck and bite.
No stars are in the sky,
no eyrie owls in flight.

vii (Lydford Gorge)

The rabbit paused, twitched ears, lolloped away
and all the woodland broke in glorious song.
My longing to go down, down, down, was strong
and yet it wasn't plausible to stay.
Bring me through sleeting rain; here I will play;
with sturdy footwear/trousers I belong.
Can seraphim, swords drawn, bar gates? So wrong,
this east of Eden. My heart sinks to lay

beside the Devil's Cauldron. Paradise
ferns at the edge, to swoop and drop, to feed
on stumbling stones and ragged panting heights.
Here is the place, a palace, fire and ice,
where Eve is dawning: there where love-lies-bleed
-ing. And there's the cloud – unknowing's new insights.

viii   (Bright Eyes)

I have bright eyes and use them every day
to catch a glimpse of tail or twisting ear
and yet there never is that lurking fear
that, tremoring with torpor, it won't stay.
For in the cotton wool, my pen will play
with every nuance of its bob-bright; clear
as blades of grass, forget-me-nots, a spear
of St Teresa's agonies, that flay

my spirits into cloudburst, bleeding gold.
My pulse would ruby finger-pricks, to write
and spin new spiders' webs till flesh turns cold.
There's ecstasy in scribbling dark to light;
there's twitching in a whisker's breadth, so bold;
there's heaven when green grazing's poised in flight.

ix (Senryu)

The window cleaner
wipes and foams and rubs, pretends
he cannot see in

x (Haiku)

Plane trees are twitching
each leaf beneath a grey sky;
branches barely sway

xi (Lord Of...) (Tanka)

The fly buzzes off
and back again in darting
chance; to buzz on by,
beyond the bonsai tree; still
his buzzing stiff as silence.

xii (Devil's Cauldron) (Tetractys)

The
Devil's
Cauldron roars,
thunders, echoes
and bubbles like first Paradise reborn.

xiii (Coffee Break) (Cinquain)

Coffee
on the table,
a luxury sinking
into leather sofa, to read;
pure bliss.

xiv (Leaving Lydford) (Minimal Davidian)

When heaven has arrived, it's time to leave
and I can't rearrange my calm, nor rush
to meetings, chores and all that makes me grieve
for loss – for just a day – of such great hush.
And that is heaven; fallen.

xv (Sunset)

And now the strangest day breaks, in the world,
with vividness of sunlight on the moor,
spread out with summer greens and earth, before
the scorching wilt of blooms, just now unfurled.
There's nothing new, my flesh is foetal-curled
and nothing seems as simple, nor as sure.
I drop, umbilical, in nature's flaw,
unknitted in my bones and sinews, purled

beyond the greatest price a shell can prove
by nacred grief that does not flow, not yet
and who knows if it ever will. To face
the cost – in heart and mind – for there was love,
unconsecrated and full of regret.
You've gone, my sister, to another place.

(xviib Senryu)

Taken from side ward,
too hot; can't breathe; so gather
round, but much too late

xvi (Hamlet's Father)

I have to concentrate to stay alive
and so my brain must still, so it can sleep.
And yet great drifting's too much, and so deep.
I need to pause in slumbering, to drive.
I hope to keep alert, so I arrive
refreshed beyond all Devon air, to keep
faith with my family, yet I could sweep
mountains under carpets, and so deprive

dreams, ghosts and nightmares of their centre stage.
I'm standing in the wings, I dare not lie
with past nor future's present, that will walk
like Hamlet's father. How to turn the page
into tomorrow; chapters pass me by,
for – in my nightmares – ghosts can also talk.

xvii (The Going is Easy)

It's early and the going doesn't get
any easier. A long slow
dawning, where the sky is grey
and who knows what rolls in
to storm and shout.

It doesn't get any easier than this,
to be taken ill and then to be taken
before the ambulance arrives.
Many things that could be said or thought
and yet, none of them get any easier
than this.

xviii (Yesterday)

Yesterday. All my troubles seemed so here to stay.
Yesterday, none of them were far away.
Yesterday, I knew what they were.
Yesterday, they were there, not here.
So, yesterday is the only place
I can make sense of your absent face.
No, I don't believe in yesterday.
No, I don't believe they will go away.

xix (Too Soon)

Now there is a chill in the morning air
and it's far too early to make a noise.
Yet there is nothing left, there is no choice;
this hotel room is a tomb to nowhere.
I brew the steaming coffee, loud, unfair,
the pouring reassuring, with no poise.
A teaspoon chinking, water splashed, no voice,
not here, not there, not now nor anywhere.

Liquid tremors, vapour rises; it's so dark.
Thick curtains have shut out the morning light.
And it's too late to catch a whiff of sleep;
to walk wild Dartmoor, hear the morning lark;
to shy from ponies that have taken fright;
to think of secrets only dead men keep.

xx (Fruit of the Tree)

A hard time we had of it, growing up
and the eldest shouldered the full weight
of responsibility at the core.
When the worm turns, it doesn't yet appear
what we will be.
The future's a messy divorce
from the past.
And everything unknowable is more so now;
there are no questions left,
                              nor anyone to answer.

xxi (Leaving)

My eyes are dry as the earth,
my face is plain as the sea.
My skin is stretched on a skull.
This day is a new day to me.

There's cars on the road in to town.
There's food at my door, food to eat.
The dregs of my drink are now chill.
This room's full of light and a seat.

Each twitch of my watch has passed slow
and soon, so remote, in TV,
my mind will be lost in the trash.
What news, for today, is for me?

I shower and dress and pack.
I pull the blinds, I will see.
My case I take to the car.
If I leave; or stay; it is me.

xxii (Tea Party)

If I could live as meek as life demands
I would be dead. A hard rain's falling now.
And I am drained and leeched, I have no power
to pulse and flow and make. It all compounds
into a tea party. Dormouse in a pot
and I will never pour myself again.
There's nothing there. The tale is just a name
with whiskers and a top hat. Lottery.

So shall we gather round? Or drink, or drown?
Do paperwork? How fast the world moves on.
I can only see a black cat and blancmange.
What will I do, or leave? What would I own?
I hope they will fight tooth and nail; when gone.
My words are free, and all of them are orange.

xxiii (Dartmoor)

On the line was a call centre,
it rang insistently and long.
I needed a friend or mentor,
on the line was a call centre.
One moment, I flashed past Brentor...
there, to be there, where I belong.
I needed a friend or mentor,
on the line was a call centre.

xxiv (Awake, it's Morning)

And now we're on our way, yet are not there,
nor ever will be, although on the way.
There never will be, now, another day
when there's a strong-brewed tea that we can share.
There is no family I shall compare:
so like a winter's tale; you're now away
where only dregs are poured out; waste to stay.
A compost heap with teabags, beyond repair.

Infuse me with the essence of fresh brew;
and warm the pot and let it stew quite well;
set out best china, chink and stir and pour.
The tray is laid out. Why are there so few?
To count out cups; what stories they could tell.
Awake; it's morning. We're drained dry some more.

xxv (Bring on the Clowns)

Life is a journey; here's a mystery,
how could I pick up pen to write it down,
a somersaulting wheeling circus clown?
He's cycling round with great temerity
in circles in the ring – again I see –
the elephant is trampling through the town
so many ways that sea lions flap and drown;
it's time to mask the mirror that is me,

and now the lion roars and maims and prowls;
the high trapeze has zipped across the market;
the strong man/dancing girls all leave en masse;
and now a Siamese twin hacks, splits and howls;
a truck's slow puncture bleeds, so we must park it.
Bring back the clowns; life is a Mardi Gras.

17

xxvi (The Never-Ending Tor) (Sestina)

There is a road to nowhere in us all,
it never ends, it rises or it sinks.
Climbing to the top, it is a lighthouse
with all of heaven and earth spread out beneath.
And then, the deepest mine's descending train
to subterranean lake, without a breath.

Waking up each day, to chance each breath
that's natural as life and in us all,
our feelings – birds – we cannot catch the train
until the pouncing cat, and all hope sinks.
We dare not look what gift there, lies beneath
its paws. We climb the spiral stairs: a lighthouse.

The light beams out to sea,   from the lighthouse.
We sit inside round rooms to snuggle breath
with one cat on our lap. What lies beneath
this bedrock on the tide? Storm-lashed by all
tsunamis – falling, falling, toppling, sinks.
The ocean calms, all-glistering its train.

It steams up Snowdon's majesty, a train
beyond each beacon, far below, or lighthouse.
With ragged breath, my clambering heart now sinks,
where mountain air thins into final breath.
What dwarf reaches the skies, to see it all?
A mortal coil that tugs us down beneath

all heaven and hell. Icarus is beneath
the scorching sun; its rays wax/wane our train
to glory, when we try to stand up tall.
The Hoe remains. This journey, as a lighthouse.
There's candle-holders, lanterning each breath
for pilgrims/fathers. A Titanic sinks.

Dressed for culture: toilets, baths and sinks,
we live, we die, we travel on beneath.
All joy and sorrow's born of final breath.
The journey's short. When is the final train?
Spring tides so high. A new moon on the lighthouse.
The keeper's gone now; such a narrow hall.

A heart sinks as we listen for the train,
to guard beneath the waves of Pluto's lighthouse.
We take first breath; a sailor's drowning call.

xxvii (Gathering of the Clans)

There's fallout every way I look; and grief
as individual as each one receives
the news and consequences for each life's belief
and only one, a poet, now conceives

that there is more than the sum of all its parts.
Strange unconsidered consequences ghost
beyond the moment's tears and loving hearts.
The cry is all humanity's great host

of witnesses. To gather round; to mourn
for all they now forget. To show respect
we silence every one; like sheep, new-shorn;
united – hidden briefly – so connect

with absence that, beloved, none else can fill
and, for a moment, warring thaws to thrill.

xxviii (Lucky Cat)

I was your bridesmaid once, that first time round
when you were Swinging Sixties up the aisle.
How aspirations grew from youth, to found
the bedrock of my adult wish-list, file

'to have and hold', blancmange-like, in your train
and gaze amazed at sapphire/diamond ring.
My turquoise gown, fluffed hat and muff, it's plain,
were elemental futures that would bring

a black cat dangled from a wrist; so posed
and someone giving lucky horseshoe; faux.
And now there's nothing; this bride is a ghost;
genes search through debris. Why? Where did she go,

so no source now remembers, or can tell
what knowledge; what surmised; of luck, of hell.

ADDENDUM

PICTURE FRAMED

You want my heart. You really want my heart?
You would not like my heart; there are no words
that I could write, beneath all heaven, with scope to paint
the universe in just the shade you want.

You think I could write words like you, to find
that we have hearts that beat the same.
There lives a universe within this throbbing skull
and would you wish the gates of hell unleashed?

You want my heart, to gently cry
and mop away your own tears and your pain.
You want connections that can pound
the ocean to the shore - as driftwood, formed,

complete perfection of the stars that shine
and glistering of moist skin, buffed so smooth.
And then you'd close that paper, put away
into a drawer marked 'Mementos'. You, not me.

These words - everyone - they are what you see.

IF (Shakespearian sonnet)

If there is heaven and hell, she is in hell
and yet her life was so; so can it be
that in the afterlife, that all is well?
All manner of things, maybe, that I can't see.

If there is nothing more; she is at peace,
a corpse without a future, and no past
that can be quiet or happy, when griefs cease
to be remembered. Her sins were so vast

that, Bowderstone, I climb up for the view
and nothing – but an Ice Age – melts my heart
to Derwentwater, flooding and so true
as you, my sister; your rock must depart

so I can calmly row out on the lake.
And then, in peace, my soul can Break; Break; Break.

Note: inspired by 'The Darkling Thrush' Thomas Hardy

TIME! (Shakespearian sonnet)

It's true I am the one that didn't die,
not this time – nor the next, perhaps – I live
and breathe, enjoy each new day passing by.
You don't have grace to see this glass; forgive.

I will not get blind drunk and share the pain,
nor pour out all the dregs a barrel's known.
You think that sediment cannot remain,
if silence fails to broadcast and atone.

I never will treat you as my best friend;
it's far too late to speak, or share, or grieve.
And so, each stalemate calls on Time's dead-end,
you think that closing time can help relieve

this water into wine; the gutter's foul.
Leave me alone where grapes of wrath will howl.

HICKLING BROAD (Shakespearian sonnet)

A host of greylags cackling on the water,
swans spooning in the shallows of the mere.
A drift of hire boats, channel marking greener
than shallow draughts and sails where flappings steer.

A page of passing plane fumes cross the sky,
as broad as Norfolk's gentler shades of blue.
The engine chugs along, as spirits fly
vibrations, to the dense of deepest brew.

Unnumbered and unrecognised, they flit
like lords and ladies, fluttering in reeds.
Swifts dance, far overhead; landlubbers sit
with mobile phones, zoom lens, entrancing reads.

My soul is fendered where swan wherries sail;
I gaze where dragonflies of dreams impale.

PARTING WORDS (Petrarchan sonnet)

Some things are unforgiveable, once known,
like how you raged and raged and caused such pain,
that gave me no recourse. Let feelings drain
so I could not redress; pick up the phone.
You shamed me in the family; each bone
disjointed, I could not face that again.
I had to cut off contact; so insane;
your past was haunting. Now I'm left alone.

Who could have risked your vengeance, like the tide?
And so I did not visit her; your haste
deprived me of a sister who I miss,
and you, half-brother, are an ocean wide.
Impassable, perhaps, and such a waste.
Some things are unforgiveable; not this.

CARDS ON THE MANTELPIECE (Petrarchan sonnet)

The cards are lined up on the mantelpiece
proclaiming celebrations and a date
significant and final. What a wait
for party and for presents and to please
-pick up the phone, it's ringing- time to tease
youthful exuberance. Let's celebrate!
This only happens once, no cards are late,
they're full of happiness and family peace.

And soon they will be put away; you'll leave
and one, now two cards peep through like faint stars
of graver news; unplanned; and warped to strains,
gargantuan as planet shifts. We'll grieve
your college date. Fools mourning life's cold farce
and whether empty cards fill what remains.

SLEEPING

You want it all – today – so you can sleep
beneath collective consciousness, so deep
that you need never fear to wake again,
if this is bliss, to sleep and die quite plain.

You want to hear – tonight – that all is well
within that ocean of our nacred shell?
You want that orange falling from the tree,
beneath my chin, dripped with sincerity?

You want the truth screamed from the highest hill,
that leaves my lungs? And leaves, and LEAVES me still?
You want a shock to lounge your afternoons
with rhythm, blues, and jazz, for folk, too soon.

If I give you all this, your soul and mine,
what pain will turn the key to shut out time?
Your eyes, as sieves, will pour the ocean dry
and then you will not need to ask me, Why?

Inspired by 'Sharing' by Kay Weeks

ABSENCE

The sun is shining in the sky
you failed to tell, except when she had died.
The blackbirds flow in liquid praise
your party invites shared, and others placed.
The garden buds to hallowed bloom
your funeral arrangements should come sooner.
The jay displays a masquerade
your open grief will leave mine ungraded.
The nightingale sings for me, may
exclude me, just like you, again, again.

THE DATE (sonnet)

Goodbye, you have to leave now for awhile,
I soak up moments like it is the end.
I recognise your every frown or smile,
and each memento that I comprehend

is shot through heart or lens. Who could erase
each precious memory stored against time.
Your daily absence, present in each place,
and my arms ache for visits, grown sublime.

Goodbye, it is like any other day,
the day you did not choose to die, the same
first bloom and fall of precious absent May
that blossoms like a stillborn. What remains?

Goodbyes and memories; why, sister, share
this timelessness; this date that's so unfair.

DEAF (Shakespearian sonnet)

The old man's life has teetered on the edge
and garbled in translation's megaphone.
Bad news can travel slowly into knowledge,
like plopping in the water, mud, a stone

sinks unexpectedly to tetchy flow
and it's too murky to hear ageing sound.
'She's gone.' 'Where to?' The world's too fast to show
downstream's a ferryman, dim eyes have found

wise to avoid. And we, what did we hear?
Death in the family. It seemed so sure
and yet, such news is never what we fear.
She's gone. He teeters to the funereal-flaw

And every phone that rings too loud, too long,
leaves us shouting;   teetering and wrong.

FUNERAL ARRANGEMENTS

I considered what to write, if a eulogy
was called for. But I was met with
riotous thoughts, and the silence
that would never be present, if I dared
to speak. What could be said, what
couldn't? A honeymoon baby,
where relatives puzzled over dates
and found nothing scandalous.
Nothing beyond parental marriage,
shotgun grandparents, and
relationships. It would be unwise
to speak further. A child of rationing,
growing up in the Swinging Sixties.
Free love? Who knows. Blackpool featured
largely. Except, choice of words is always
inappropriate. And I can never forget
bragging, the first time I was an Aunty,
nor considered practical issues like
who was the father? Who worked,
who was left holding the baby?
I knew who washed the Terries nappies,
dumped behind Grandad's sofa
after each visit.
It would be unwise to speak of the blushing bride,
looking like Priscilla Presley marrying Elvis,
cutting the cake on Valentine's Day
and delivering her black cat and horseshoe
baby a few months later. It would be unwise
to speak further. To consider a perfect
mirror image cremation: of a son
and now a mother. The gathering
of family grievances, long-recognised faces.
Nor to look in the mirror and hope
I don't grow more like my sister every day.
Silence is needed here. Even growing has
unintended meanings; when men are absent
or inadequate; to fathering? To marriage?

To my sister? A weighty silence
must be avoided at all costs. There must be
no mention of cause of death; nor cyberspace;
nor who married who and when; nor whether
there was a marriage? birth? death? (again, and again, and...)
To eulogise would be unwise.
Ordering flowers was easy;
the funeral directors have none of the details,
being met with silence, ministers attempting to contact relatives.
Their telephone manner (politely)? Efficient.

THE FUNERAL

Family gathered at the flat,
and time passed, like a lifetime,
flashing before their eyes.
Arrivals, no departures
and everyone's words dressed
politely in black, absorbing light.

Nothing happened until that first cigarette,
lined up along the balcony, watching the world
arrive, a shade of silver with famous insignia.
None mentioned the earth opening up
to swallow grieving whole.

The professionals dressed
as smart as England: top hat, tails,
carrying a black cane
leading the entourage in its wake.

Contd over...

THE FUNERAL contd

Music beat loudly from the neighbourhood
and who could tell whether anyone
paused to stare. Lights dipped,
a cortege in convoy. Don't stop dead.
Follow the rules of the road:
traffic lights on red, motorbikes snaking
ahead, polished saloons queue-jumping,
caught in a grief-ridden sandwich
stop-start-stop-start... lurching ahead
to the Crem.

Everyone crowded around, unrehearsed,
as weighty unloading, wheeling of casualty
carried on in silence.
Guide dogs, packed in with white sticks.
The aged wobbled on walking sticks
and no-one stared a moment too long,
wondering when, awake or sleeping,
some would gather again; too soon.
Or not. Long-lost relatives crowded
into chapel. Greeting and grabbing
favourite hands, strategic seats.

The minister rose on a wave of grief,
calmly negotiated ceasefire, for a day.
Light, bright and horribly stuffy,
none creaked or shifted weight.

The presence finely encased in wood,
strategically placed wreaths, an alphabet
spelt out MUM.

Guests learnt the abacus of a life,
diplomatically retold to avoid offence.
None were forgotten, excluded,
a eulogy anyone could wear proudly,
in absentia. Shoulders rubbed, that would
never touch again. Grief trickling
or pounding down each cheek
to a full crescendo of grief.

Culminating in 'The Lord's My Shepherd'
and The Lord's Prayer (traditional).
Everyone fell outside quickly,
after the final curtain.
The show was over; closing night.
And if the minister whispered prayers,
clutching the hand of a deaf old man
seated and barely nodding off at the end,
it was a fine effort.

The sun shone; wreathes arranged themselves
for photographs, along with family members
who could laugh, hug, exchange contact details.
Smoke spewed out in all directions;
none dragged away from the group.
Someone attempted an ad-hoc sermon,
that fell on deaf ears (the old man's).
And, like a tide, they ebbed away
to a wake. A train to catch. Dinner to cook.
The silence of mile on mile of uniform tarmac,
like a funeral. And one old man, alone,
dozing in front of the TV.

A WHERRY LONG TIME AGO (pantoum)

It was the best day of our lives, afloat
across the broad of Hickling's beauteous sky.
In tiny hired motorised cabined boat,
I leant back, staring, as the world flowed by.

Across the broad of Hickling's beauteous sky,
my memories were freshly beached to row.
I leant back, staring as the world flowed by.
Last time seemed one year, not eighteen, ago.

My memories were freshly beached. To row
was then, as now, absurd. I lay to see
last time seemed one year, not eighteen, ago
and now, here was a strapping lad with me.

Was then, as now, absurd? I lay, too sea
within my flesh, while here a brother grew
and now, here was a strapping lad with me,
nonchalant with youth that can help Dad crew.

Within my flesh, while here a brother grew,
I now watch Marbled Whites dance in the reeds.
Nonchalant with youths that can help Dad crew,
I wherry dragonflies where water leads.

I now watch Marbled Whites dance in the reeds.
In tiny hired motorised cabined boat,
I wherry dragonflies where water leads.
It was the best day of our lives, afloat.

HEARTS AND FLOWERS

Nothing appears to sing
the tune of all creation in my choices.
Picking up plants and putting them down,
loving one, hating another.
Cannot concentrate on fade or fall,
over-watering, aridly ignored
never dying.

Choosing sunshine and fruit:
strawberries in June,
blooms a shade of girlie pink,
sunflower in pot
to trace hours and shine
in endless glistering summer.

Nothing chosen has more
nor less heart, sitting in the bar
listening to rhythm and blues
and letting beer slide down smoothly.
When was relaxing this easy?

Girls on a night out, one husband
for chauffeur. Earlier, much earlier,
a bakery delight, as words tumbled
a lifetime in one hour.

Tomorrow, I am not myself
among flowers, chattering
like a sparrow among many crumbs

of cold comfort, in the wake of silence.
Except, later, much later, before the day is through

driving home; kindness blooming in the heart.

Inspired by 'Resemblances' by Kay Weeks

AFTER HEAVY RAINS

It seems that we are greater than we know
for all of life has gathered in this moment
and, no matter what the circumstances,
the floodtide concentrates to a stream
through narrowed rock.

And now I see the waterfall of praise
for every human flowing over bridges
and crowds, and crowds of memories
come crowding in at the last.
Who will listen? What will speak?
It is not yet known what we will become
and yet the culmination of all of life
is to twitch ancestral bones,

until they bleed and water floods the desert.
Just so, your children's children will speak,
and all the rocks will cry out to be heard
if your dam's blocked in silence.

Ancestral bones are twitching towards
the earth. So still them now,
they point beneath. And all the woodland
singing, winging, bringing the thrilling
fall-out of knowledge.

Everyone excuses themselves,
for love, for youthfulness, for distance
or for stress. None speaks with another's eyes,
and yet, all eyes show their ancestors,
and smiles and faces, tone of voice or gait.
We are what we seem. And yet, no-one knows
like others see them. Visible as a floodtide,
with no excuses left to wake a riverbed.

Humanity lives, and loves,
protects its children, or not;
its tribe, or not;
its earth, or not.
Each human voice crying loudly at the last,
a waterfall of praise.

ADDENDUM II (Extract)
ANOTHER PRELUDE by Wendy Webb

100

It happened when I was young as the hills,
for I was a 100 years old,
the time when all the world was singing
and ringing my name alive again
with the joy of all creation.

It was my last year, when I was young,
almost before I took first breath
and there, on the horizon, a white horse
galloping away.

It was no time at all, for in all things was my breath
and everything was living in that moment.
I was as young as everything
and all things were in me, for I was born.

There was no other way that I could be,
torn screaming from the wall
to bleed and cry.

It was my first word, breathless adoration.

Where was I then? Where am I now?
For everything was there, since the Big Bang.
And nothing could be any other way.

The breasts of earth bled milk
and so I drank.
But never could I quench away my thirst,
for everything was living, it was plain
as passing milk and suckling dirt,
it lived.

And so did I, to scream another day
beside the river, flowing like the Trent,
where crowds flowed over, under, every day.
And never did I ask why I was old,
to live a 100 years in just one day

nor why forget-me-nots were not born there
to bloom away my springtime in September.
For I was such a little thing, a palm
that held all sky and sea and rang, like home.

Yet there I was, I lived, I breathed, I grew
to be less ageful in a few short days.

*

99
I'm growing moments younger with each breath
and every second's such a little death
to be so bright and darksome as the earth.

Where am I now? Where was I then?
I knew so much, beyond encyclopaedic knowledge:
I could write with every breath I spoke,
I learned it all.

For everything was in that moment – born –
and nothing was then hid from my blue eyes.
I opened wide the world that spread each day
and tasted all life brought, I was so young
as any other way, as day and night.
All things were breathed in moments, understood.
The white horse galloped off, it could not stay
beyond the far horizon where I slept.

For I was 99 and then a day,
but nothing more was left except the silence.
I cried it out, night after night,
and no-one there translated what it meant.